MONARCH BUTTERFLIES

by Josh Gregory

Children's Press®

An Imprint of Scholastic Inc.

Content Consultant
Dr. Stephen S. Ditchkoff
Professor of Wildlife Ecology and Management
Auburn University
Auburn, Alabama

Photographs ©: cover: Joel Sartore/National Geographic Creative;
1: Gregg Williams/Dreamstime; 2, 3: Jostein Hauge/Dreamstime; 4,
5 background: Frans Lanting/Getty Images; 5 top: Animals Animals/
Superstock, Inc.; 5 bottom: Brigitte Smith/Getty Images; 7: Brian
Overcast/Alamy Images; 8: David Aubrey/Media Bakery; 10, 11:
Gregg Williams/Dreamstime; 12, 13: Gillian Hardy/Dreamstime;
15: Papilio/Alamy Images; 16, 17: Melinda Fawver/Dreamstime;
19: age fotostock/Superstock, Inc.; 20, 21: Raul Gonzalez/Science
Source; 23: Animals Animals/Superstock, Inc.; 24, 25: Frans Lanting/
Getty Images; 26, 27: Paul A. Zahl/National Geographic/Getty
Images; 28: Doug Wechsler/age fotostock; 30, 31: Michael Kern/
Getty Images; 32, 33: Madozi/Dreamstime; 35: Howard Cheek/
Dreamstime; 36, 37: Brigitte Smith/Getty Images; 38, 39: Tony Hertz/
Alamy Images; 40, 41: steve bly/Alamy Images; 44, 45: Jostein
Hauge/Dreamstime; 46: Gregg Williams/Dreamstime.

Library of Congress Cataloging-in-Publication Data
Gregory, Josh, author.
  Monarch butterflies / by Josh Gregory.
  pages cm. — (Nature's children)
  Summary: "This book details the life and habits of monarch
butterflies"— Provided by publisher.
  Includes bibliographical references and index.
  ISBN 978-0-531-22722-0 (library binding : alk. paper) — ISBN 978-
0-531-22520-2 (pbk. : alk. paper)
  1. Monarch butterfly—Juvenile literature. I. Title. II. Series: Nature's
children (New York, N.Y.)
  QL561.D3G74 2016
  595.78'9—dc23   2015020025

Printed in China 62
SCHOLASTIC, CHILDREN'S PRESS, and associated logos are
trademarks and/or registered trademarks of Scholastic Inc.

2 3 4 5 6 7 8 9 10 R 25 24 23 22 21 20 19 18 17 16

Monarch Butterflies

Class	Insecta
Order	Lepidoptera
Family	Nymphalidae
Genus	*Danaus*
Species	*Danaus plexippus*
World distribution	Primarily found in North, Central, and South America; also found in Australia, India, and sometimes other locations
Habitat	Forests, grasslands, and mountains
Distinctive physical characteristics	Four wings with orange, black, and white markings; wingspan is around 3.5 to 4 inches (9 to 10 centimeters); narrow, black body is around 1 inch (2.5 cm) long; six legs; two antennae; caterpillars grow up to around 2.75 inches (7 cm) long and have black, white, and yellow stripes along their bodies
Habits	Monarchs living in areas with cold winters migrate each year to avoid cold temperatures; those in warmer climates stay put year-round; wintering monarchs often gather in huge groups on trees; lays eggs exclusively on milkweed plants
Diet	Adult monarchs feed on the nectar of flowers; caterpillars eat leaves, buds, and juice of milkweed plants

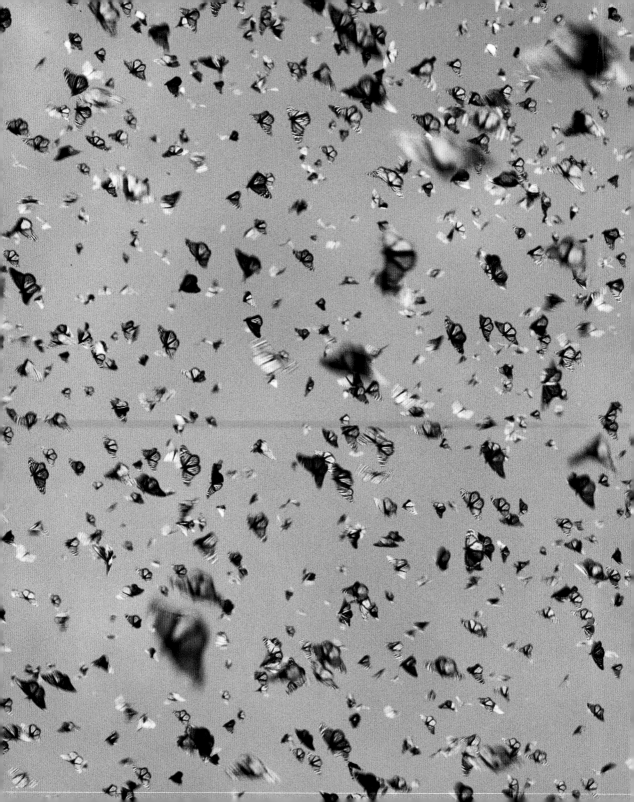

Contents

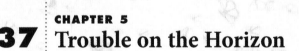

CHAPTER 1

Bunches of Butterflies

The sun shines down on a beautiful afternoon in the mountains of western Mexico. Though it is the middle of February, the weather remains fairly warm and bright here. Thanks to the pleasant weather, there is plenty of activity in the dense plant growth of this mountain forest. Even the huge oyamel fir trees that cover much of the hillside seem to be in motion.

The trees' leaves and branches are not simply swaying in the breeze, however. They are covered in a thick layer of monarch butterflies! The butterflies' beautiful black-and-orange wings seem to cover every bit of the trees. They flutter from the bottom of the tree trunks up to the highest branches. There are countless butterflies clustered together on each tree. They have flown thousands of miles from their homes in the United States and Canada. Now they will spend the winter in Mexico's sunshine.

Monarch butterflies often cluster together so closely on a tree that it can be impossible to see the tree itself.

Tiny Creatures

Monarch butterflies are not very large creatures. These insects have narrow, black bodies that measure about 1 inch (2.5 centimeters) from head to tail. Attached to a monarch's back are two pairs of wings. When fully extended, the wingspan is between 3.5 and 4 inches (9 and 10 cm). Each butterfly weighs just 0.0095 to 0.026 ounces (0.27 to 0.74 grams). That is so lightweight you probably wouldn't notice if a butterfly was resting on your arm.

A butterfly also has six long, thin legs it uses to walk and climb on a variety of surfaces. On its head, there are two antennae to help it sense its surroundings. Butterflies have powerful eyes that they use to recognize the patterns on the wings of other butterflies. Their eyes also allow them to search out colorful flowers to land on.

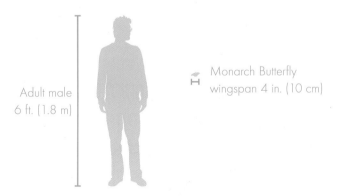

Adult male
6 ft. (1.8 m)

Monarch Butterfly
wingspan 4 in. (10 cm)

A butterfly is so light that its weight can be supported by a delicate flower.

Wondrous Wings

A butterfly's large, brightly colored wings are by far its most noticeable feature. Every butterfly species has unique patterns and colors on its wings. A monarch's wings are mainly orange. Black lines divide the orange into smaller sections. There is also a thick line of black along the edge of each wing with rows of white markings. The orange color on the topside of the wings is very bright. The color is a darker, brownish tint on the underside.

Butterfly wings are very thin. They are formed from a material called chitin. This substance also forms human hair and fingernails. Covering the chitin of a butterfly's wings is a layer of tiny scales. These scales give the wings their color. Butterfly scales are very delicate. If you have ever touched a butterfly, you may have noticed a powdery substance on your fingers afterward. This powder is actually butterfly scales!

FUN FACT! The black markings on a female monarch's wings are usually thicker than the ones on a male.

A monarch's beautiful wings make it easy to spot in a field of flowers.

A Monarch's Home

Depending on the time of year, monarch butterflies can be found throughout huge portions of North, Central, and South America. They live in a wide variety of habitats. You might find them clustered together in a forest or fluttering about in a grassy field. You can also spot monarchs flying high on a mountain or among the weeds alongside a busy road. You may even notice them in your own backyard. They range from southern Canada south to the northern regions of South America. In addition to their American homes, monarchs are found in parts of Australia and India.

One place you won't find monarch butterflies is in the middle of a snowstorm. Monarchs cannot survive in cold temperatures. To thrive, they need warm temperatures and large, wild areas filled with a variety of plants.

Forests are one of the many types of habitats that monarchs make their home.

CHAPTER 2

Going Through Changes

Monarch butterflies have a complex life cycle. From birth to adulthood, their bodies go through several major changes. As a result, a newly hatched monarch **larva** looks very different from a full-grown monarch.

The process begins when a male and female monarch **mate**. Males have special black spots on their rear wings. These spots release a scent when the male butterflies are ready to mate. Females detect the scent in the air and follow it to the male. The pair then flies down to the ground to mate.

Soon after a male and female monarch mate, the female is ready to lay eggs. Monarchs lay their eggs one at a time, attaching them to the bottoms of leaves on milkweed plants. Each egg is roughly the size of a pinhead. It is a yellowish-green color and is shaped somewhat like a football with one flat end.

Monarch eggs have a ridged texture.

A Larva's Lifestyle

A larva, or caterpillar, hatches about four days after an egg is laid.
A newly hatched monarch caterpillar is extremely small. Its body
is about 0.2 inches (5 millimeters) long. It is very narrow, with
several sets of legs. It is completely white except for a black head.
It also has two pairs of bumps on its back. One pair is located at
each end of the caterpillar.

The caterpillar spends its time eating the same milkweed
plant it hatched on. It consumes leaves, flower buds, and any other
plant bit available. This food helps the caterpillar grow. During
its first two weeks, the caterpillar molts five times. Each time, it
sheds a layer of skin to reveal a new layer underneath. This allows
the caterpillar to grow rapidly. The caterpillar's appearance also
changes with each molt. It develops a pattern of yellow, black, and
white stripes along its body. The bumps on its back grow longer. By
the caterpillar's last molt, it is about 2.75 inches (7 cm) long. That is
14 times its length when it first hatched!

Caterpillars move slowly and spend most of their time eating.

From Caterpillar to Chrysalis

Once the caterpillar reaches its full size, it begins preparing for the next stage of its life. In just a few minutes, the caterpillar will change its shape entirely. First, it searches out a sturdy twig or leaf that can support its weight. Then it produces a sticky material called silk. It uses the silk to attach its back end to the twig. Hanging upside down, the caterpillar then sheds its skin one more time. Now the monarch's **pupa** stage is visible. This is also called a chrysalis.

The chrysalis is a light green color, and it is dotted with small yellow marks. The exterior is smooth. It does not have any visible body parts sticking out. Inside, the monarch is changing. Over the course of about two weeks, an adult monarch butterfly forms inside the chrysalis. It soon becomes possible to see the monarch's orange-and-black wings through the outer layer of the chrysalis.

If you look carefully, you can see a monarch's wing pattern developing inside this chrysalis.

Life as a Butterfly

When its development is complete, the adult monarch breaks free from its chrysalis. It is able to fly almost immediately. Now it can begin the adult monarch's daily routine of feeding and searching for mates. Monarch butterflies feed by flying from flower to flower in search of the sugary nectar inside. They use a long, narrow body part called a **proboscis** to suck up the nectar. They drink water the same way.

Adult monarchs have a built-in defense against most **predators**. The milkweed that monarch caterpillars feed on contains substances that taste bad to many animals. These substances remain in the monarch's body during its **metamorphosis** into a butterfly. Over time, most predators have learned to avoid monarchs because of their bad taste. However, some predators are resistant to this defense. Rats and certain kinds of birds are among the deadly animals that monarchs try to avoid.

A monarch's proboscis curls up when it is not in use.

Not Long-Lived

Most monarch butterflies do not live very long. Those born in the spring or early summer have an adult life span of just four to five weeks. The same is true of monarchs that live in areas with warm weather all year long. During this short time, the butterflies do their best to mate and reproduce before they die. If a butterfly is born in spring, its great-grandchildren will likely be born before the end of summer the same year.

Many monarchs live in places with cold winters. These populations consist of one **generation** each year that has a much longer life span. These butterflies can live up to eight or nine months. They use this time to make an epic journey from northern and eastern areas to Mexico or California. They spend the winter months there before beginning a return trip in the spring.

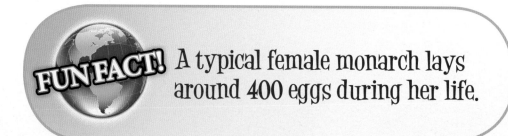

FUN FACT! A typical female monarch lays around 400 eggs during her life.

Butterflies living in Hawaii stay in the same place all year long.

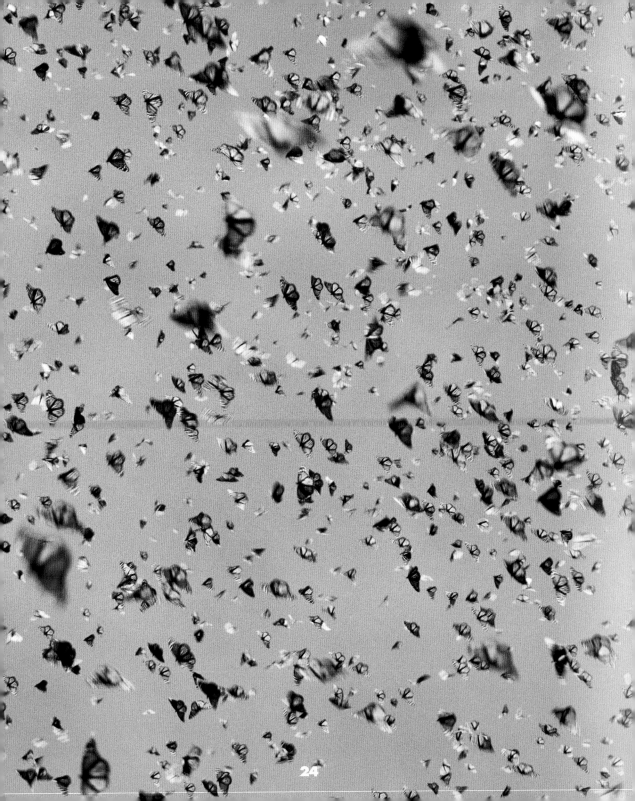

CHAPTER 3

The Long Journey

Monarchs begin their **migration** in early fall, when the weather is not yet too cold. Depending on where a monarch begins, it might travel as far as 3,000 miles (4,828 kilometers). Monarchs migrate in large groups. They only fly during the day, when temperatures are warmer. At night, they huddle together in trees to stay warm. As the sun rises the next morning, the monarchs absorb its warmth before they continue their journey.

Not all monarchs migrate. These butterflies live in places that stay warm all year, such as Puerto Rico, India, and Hawaii. There, monarchs continue the cycle of rapid reproduction and short life spans no matter the time of year.

FUN FACT! Migrating monarchs have larger wings and bodies than those that live in the same place year-round.

Huge groups of butterflies travel together on their yearly migration.

There and Back Again

Migrating monarchs usually arrive at their destination sometime in October. All migrating monarchs travel to the same dozen or so locations in Mexico and California for the winter. In California, the butterflies stay along the coast of the Pacific Ocean. In Mexico, they seek out forests that grow high up in the mountains. There, they gather on the branches and trunks of oyamel fir trees. Though the weather here is warm, the butterflies must still remain close together to conserve body heat. During this time, they do not sip nectar or search for mates. They simply wait for spring to come.

Around March, the monarchs begin the long journey home. Along the way, they start mating and laying eggs across Texas and the plains to the north and east. Once these eggs hatch and the metamorphosis is complete, these new butterflies continue along the path their parents were traveling. Eventually, monarchs reach their summer homes throughout the United States and Canada.

Some butterflies spend the winter along the Pacific coast in California.

Finding the Way

No one is entirely sure how monarch butterflies know when and where to migrate. Because monarchs reproduce and die so quickly, they only ever migrate once. They do not learn from experience, and they never live long enough to show later generations how to make the trip. Monarchs are simply born with the **instinct** to migrate.

Experts believe that monarchs use several methods to **navigate**. One way is by observing the position of the sun overhead. Another method involves sensing Earth's magnetic field. This field runs through and around the planet, and magnetic compasses determine north and south by it. Along their journey, the butterflies probably communicate with one another using chemicals called **pheromones**.

FUN FACT! Sometimes, so many monarch butterflies gather on a single tree that their combined weight causes branches to break.

Scientists mark the wings of migrating butterflies with special tags that help them track the butterflies' routes.

CHAPTER 4

Incredible Insects

Monarchs, along with all other butterflies, belong to the class of animals known as insects. When you think of insects, you probably imagine troublesome pests such as roaches, ants, or mosquitoes. However, not all insects are creepy crawling and flying creatures that bother people. Many of them, including monarch butterflies, are beautiful and can even be very helpful.

Insects make up around 75 percent of all known animal species. So far, scientists have classified roughly one million different insect species. These creatures vary greatly in size, appearance, and lifestyle. Some are so small they can barely be seen with the naked eye. Others are quite large. All these animals, including butterflies, have a few things in common, however. Instead of bones, they have hard exoskeletons. Their bodies are also divided into three segments. In addition, most species have six legs and either two or four wings.

Compared with a monarch butterfly, this flower mantis's exoskeleton is very easy to see.

Learning about Lepidoptera

About 14,000 different butterfly species are living today. Together with about 150,000 moth species and 3,500 **skippers** they make up the **order** Lepidoptera. All lepidoptera share the basic life cycle of the monarch. They also have large, scale-covered wings.

Moths tend to have shorter, thicker bodies than butterflies. Their antennae are also different. A butterfly's antennae are shaped like clubs with a bulb, or knob, at the end. A moth's antennae are generally feathery. Additionally, butterflies hold their wings straight up behind them when they aren't flying. Moths hold their wings out to the side or wrap them around themselves.

Skippers have the same shorter, wider bodies as moths. However, they hold their wings the same way butterflies do. Their antennae are also more similar to a butterfly's, with a bend at the end.

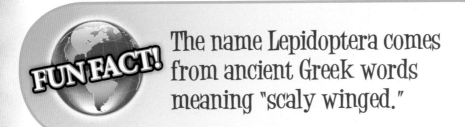

FUN FACT! The name Lepidoptera comes from ancient Greek words meaning "scaly winged."

Some moths can grow to be very large.

Colorful Copycats

The monarch has several close relatives. In fact, these butterflies are so similar they can be very difficult for the average person to tell apart. The viceroy, queen, and soldier butterflies all share a monarch's orange, black, and white coloring. Each species displays a slightly different shade of orange. Also, their white-and-black markings are shaped somewhat differently. However, it can be very difficult to spot these differences when the butterflies are on the move. Because these different species are found in many of the same areas, they are often confused for one another.

Humans aren't the only animals that have trouble telling the monarch apart from its cousins. Birds and other potential predators also seem to have difficulty distinguishing between these species. This is very helpful to the butterflies. While all of them are at least a little toxic, some taste much worse than others. Enemies tend to avoid all of them equally, however, because they can't tell which butterflies are which.

Queen butterflies look almost exactly like monarchs at first glance.

CHAPTER 5

Trouble on the Horizon

Unlike many other insects, humans generally like butterflies. A monarch's brightly colored wings are a beautiful sight, whether seen fluttering through the air or perched atop a flower. In addition, monarchs play an important role in the reproduction of flowers. When a monarch lands on a flower to sip nectar, **pollen** sticks to the butterfly's body. As the butterfly moves from flower to flower, it transfers the pollen among them. The plants rely on this transfer to create seeds to reproduce.

Unfortunately, human activities are causing big problems for these friendly insects. Because of their unique lifestyles, monarchs require very specific homes, food, and weather to survive. Yet people are affecting the world around them in a variety of ways. As the environment changes, monarchs simply will not be able to adjust fast enough. Instead, they will slowly begin to die off. Some experts even believe that monarchs could become extinct in the near future if nothing is done to help them.

Unlike many insects, monarchs do not bite, sting, or cause any other problems for humans.

Nowhere to Go

One major problem for monarchs is the disappearance of milkweed plants. Many people consider milkweed to be a nuisance. They do their best to keep it from growing in their yards, gardens, and farmland. Through the use of modern chemicals, it has become very easy for people to kill milkweed, and these plants are becoming more and more rare in the United States. Without these plants, adult monarchs have nowhere to lay their eggs, and caterpillars have nothing to eat.

Another difficulty facing monarchs is **climate change**. Winters are becoming colder and wetter in the butterflies' typical winter locations. This could cause monarchs to freeze and die.

Habitat loss is another issue affecting monarchs' winter homes. In Mexico, some of the forests where the butterflies stay are being cut down as a source of wood. In California, people are building homes and businesses in the same areas where monarchs stay.

People often clear away forests and other wild areas to build new homes, businesses, and farms.

How to Help

Organizations are working to reverse the damage to monarchs' habitats. They hope to prevent these amazing animals from dying out. Two of the largest groups are the U.S. Fish and Wildlife Service and the Monarch Joint Venture. However, you don't have to be an expert or a member of a conservation group to help. Anyone with a yard or a garden can make life easier for monarchs. Some people do this by planting milkweed. This creates a space where the insects can reproduce and go through metamorphosis. Planting flowers gives the butterflies a source of nectar after they become adults.

Search online to find out which kinds of milkweed will grow best where you live. Before long, you will probably spot butterflies and caterpillars nearby. You won't only experience the satisfaction of helping monarchs survive. You will also have the privilege of watching these incredible animals fly around your yard!

Milkweed plants can help add color to a backyard while providing homes for beautiful monarchs.

Words to Know

chitin (CHIT-ihn) — a hard substance that makes up the hard outer shell of insects, arachnids, and crustaceans

climate change (KLYE-mit CHAYNJ) — global warming and other changes in the weather and weather patterns that are happening because of human activity

conservation (kahn-sur-VAY-shuhn) — the protection of valuable things, especially forests, wildlife, natural resources, or artistic or historic objects

exoskeletons (ek-soh-SKEH-luh-tuhnz) — hard outer coverings that protect and support some animals' internal organs and muscles

generation (jen-uh-RAY-shuhn) — a group of people, animals, or other living things born around the same time

habitats (HAB-uh-tats) — places where an animal or a plant is usually found

instinct (IN-stingkt) — behavior that is natural rather than learned

larva (LAHR-vuh) — an insect at the stage of development between an egg and a pupa, when it looks like a worm

mate (MAYT) — to join together to produce babies

metamorphosis (met-uh-MOR-fuh-sis) — a series of changes some animals, such as caterpillars, go through as they develop into adults

migration (mye-GRAY-shuhn) — the movement to another area or climate at a particular time of year molts (MOHLTS) — loses old fur, feathers, or skin so that new ones can grow

navigate (NAV-i-gate) — to find where you are and where you need to go

order (OR-dur) — a group of related plants or animals that is bigger than a family but smaller than a class

pheromones (FEHR-eh-mohnz) — chemicals that animals produce to attract other animals or insects, especially to mate

pollen (PAH-luhn) — tiny yellow grains produced in the tips of flowers; pollen grains are the male cells of flowering plants

predators (PRED-uh-turz) — animals that live by hunting other animals for food

proboscis (proh-BAHS-kis) — the long, thin tube that forms part of the mouth of some insects

pupa (PYOO-puh) — an insect in an inactive stage of development between a larva and an adult

skippers (SKIHP-urz) — insects with scaled wings and stout bodies, closely related to moths and butterflies

species (SPEE-sheez) — one of the groups into which animals and plants of the same genus are divided

Habitat Map

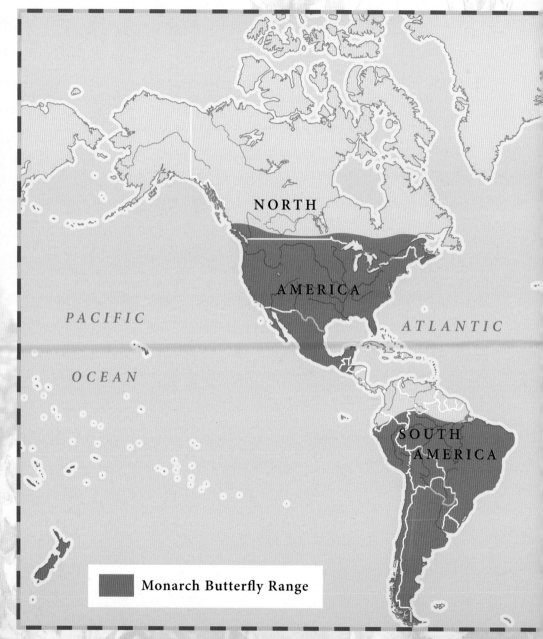

NORTH

AMERICA

SOUTH
AMERICA

PACIFIC

OCEAN

ATLANTIC

Monarch Butterfly Range

ARCTIC OCEAN

EUROPE

ASIA

AFRICA

PACIFIC OCEAN

OCEAN

INDIAN OCEAN

AUSTRALIA

Find Out More

Books

Berger, Melvin, and Gilda Berger. *Butterflies & Caterpillars*. New York: Scholastic, 2008.

Marsh, Laura F. *Butterflies*. Washington, DC: National Geographic, 2010.

Pasternak, Carol. *How to Raise Monarch Butterflies: A Step-by-Step Guide for Kids*. Buffalo, NY: Firefly Books, 2012.

Whalley, Paul. *Butterfly and Moth*. New York: DK Publishing, 2012.

Visit this Scholastic Web site for more information on monarch butterflies:
www.factsfornow.scholastic.com
Enter the keywords **Monarch Butterflies**

Index

Page numbers in *italics* indicate a photograph or map.

About the Author

Josh Gregory is the author of more than 90 books for kids. He has written about everything from animals to technology to history. A graduate of the University of Missouri–Columbia, he currently lives in Portland, Oregon.